Leaps and Bounds

David and Patricia Armentrout

Rourke
Publishing LLC
Vero Beach, Florida 32964

www.rourkepublishing.com

PHOTO CREDITS:

Editor: Kelli Hicks

Cover Design: Tara Raymo

Page Design: Renee Brady

Library of Congress Cataloging-in-Publication Data

Armentrout, David, 1962-
  Leaps and bounds / David and Patricia Armentrout.
      p. cm. -- (Weird and wonderful animals)
  ISBN 978-1-60472-304-5 (hardcover)
  ISBN 978-1-60472-801-9 (softcover)
  1. Animal jumping--Juvenile literature. I. Armentrout, Patricia, 1960- II.
Title.
  QP310.J86A76 2008
  573.7'9--dc22
                                2008019697

Printed in the USA

IG/IG

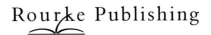

Rourke Publishing

www.rourkepublishing.com – rourke@rourkepublishing.com
Post Office Box 3328, Vero Beach, FL 32964

Table of Contents

Locomotion

Locomotion means moving from one place to another. Animals move to protect themselves, to find food, and to find a mate. Most animals, including humans, need to move to survive.

Leaping over a farmer's fence provides little challenge for this mule deer.

Wallabies have strong back legs that they use to bound quickly across long distances. But watch out! Wallabies are kangaroos kicking cousins. They are known for defending themselves by kicking with their powerful hind legs.

Leap Frog

Land animals typically walk and run. However, some creatures, big and small, can also leap and bound. In other words, some animals can spring forward quickly.

When you think of animals that leap, which ones come to mind? Frogs probably top the list. Frogs specialize in leaping.

Most frogs live in and out of water and move about by swimming and jumping.

Humans are jumpers too. The best compete in track and field sporting events.

A frog's legs are made for jumping.

Frogs are great leapers. They have short front legs and long hind legs. When they push their hind legs against the ground, energy from the push is stored in elastic **tendons**. Tendons help frogs leap further than if they used muscle power alone. Why do frogs leap? Leaping is a great way to move quickly. Frogs leap to escape **predators** and to catch **prey**.

It is hard to measure how far wild animals leap or how high they jump. People who study animal locomotion take measurements when they can and use estimates.

Kangaroos

Can you picture kangaroos hopping across the Australian Outback? Most likely, you can, because that's what kangaroos do, they hop, or move by leaps and bounds.

The length of a kangaroo's leap increases as its speed increases.

10

A kangaroo is a macropod. Macropod means large foot. Kangaroos have large, strong hind legs and feet. A kangaroo's hind legs have big stretchy tendons that help them leap into action.

Some kangaroo **species** can run faster than 40 miles per hour (64.37 km/h).

A baby kangaroo is called a joey.

Kangaroos leap to escape predators. Kangaroos also leap because it's the best way for them to move across open grasslands. Their **habitat** is huge and mostly a dry, **infertile** place. Kangaroos cover long distances when they search for food and water. Leaping allows them to do it with little effort.

Two boxing kangaroos use their tails for balance.

Purrfect Leapers

What do cougars, tigers, and even house cats have in common with frogs and kangaroos? All these animals are great jumpers.

A house cat leaps while another looks on.

Mountain lion, puma, and panther other names for cougar.

The cougar is one of the most athletic cat species. A cougar's hind legs are slightly larger than its front legs. Strong hind legs help cougars leap as high as 18 feet (5.49 meters) into trees or onto rock ledges. They also bound across the ground in leaps ranging from 20 to 40 feet (6.1 to 12.9 meters).

Leopards often take shelter in trees.

All cats are **carnivores**, and they are excellent predators. The leopard, for example, hunts just about any animal it can catch. Leopards run very fast, and can leap up to 20 feet (6.1 meters) in a single bound. They can also jump 10 feet (3.05 meters) high.

Tigers are the largest of the big cats, which include lions, leopards, and jaguars. Big cats are the only cats that can roar. Tigers are *purr*fect at using the element of surprise. They like to hide in the jungle, then stalk, leap, and bound after prey.

Tigers are an endangered species.

Antelopes

There are about 90 different kinds of antelopes, including the African impala and gazelle (also called springbok). Both are fast runners and high jumpers. When chased by a cheetah or lion, the impala leaps in different directions to confuse the predator.

The impala has a distinct "M" marking on its rear.

Impalas can jump forward more than 30 feet (9.14 meters) and leap about eight feet (2.44 meters) into the air.

Sometimes gazelles exhibit strange behavior, called stotting, when cheetahs or lions are on the hunt. They slow their running pace, arch their back, and leap high into the air. Stotting seems to make them an easy target, but the predators often leave them alone. Experts think the cats back off because the gazelles are expressing an "I'm too powerful to bother with" attitude.

The Bunny Hop

Rabbits hop when they move from place to place. Their long hind legs and big hind feet make it easy. Rabbits are born without fur, with eyes closed, and nest below ground in a burrow. Hares are similar to rabbits but they are born with fur, with eyes open, and they nest above ground.

Hares and rabbits have exceptional hearing.

20

Rabbits and hares are herbivores; they eat plants.

Hares and rabbits move in short leaps and bounds. The distance they cover between leaps is not as impressive as their speed. Hares, for example, can run 45 miles per hour (70km/h). A fast running hare is really exhibiting a series of leaps, or a gallop.

Grasshoppers

Like all insects, grasshoppers have six legs, and with the name *grasshopper*, they have to be good leapers! Grasshoppers have big, powerful hind legs that help them leap forward 20 times their length, about 30 inches (76 cm). That may not sound like much, but compare that to people power. From a standing position, many people cannot even leap forward the distance of their own height.

Long-horned grasshoppers have antennae longer than their bodies.

Grasshoppers have a hard, outside skeleton.

Grasshoppers also have wings. In fact, some species **swarm**, land on crops, and cause serious damage. If grasshoppers can fly, then why do they hop? Grasshoppers are better hoppers than flyers. They hop to escape predators like birds, lizards, and rodents (and kids with nets!).

Jumping Spiders

Jumping spiders, like all spiders, have eight legs. Their legs are not muscular like a grasshopper's, though. Jumping spiders jump because they have a special blood system that changes pressure. The pressure change causes their legs to extend. The system works so well that jumping spiders can jump up to 80 times their body length!

Jumping spiders have eight eyes. Their primary pair can see color.

Some spiders spin webs to attract and capture prey, but not jumping spiders. Jumping spiders surprise prey with a quick jump. Before an attack, a jumping spider attaches a fine silk thread to its perch. If the spider falls, it climbs back up using the thread.

Jumping spiders will often jump leaf to leaf while hunting prey.

Aquatic Leapers

Have you ever seen a giant whale rise from the ocean and then fall back with a loud slap? Scientists call this behavior **breaching**. Some species, such as the sperm whale, begin their breach in deep water. They swim straight up and rocket out of the water.

A breaching whale is an awesome sight!

26

Although there are many theories, scientists are not sure why humpback whales breach.

Humpback whales take a different approach. They pick up speed as they swim close to the surface. With one quick jerk, they leap out of the water. Imagine the enormous power it takes to drive 30 tons (30,481.41 kilograms) from the sea!

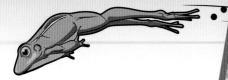

Captive dolphins
work with their trainer.

Dolphins may be the most well known **aquatic** leapers. Trainers teach these intelligent mammals to do tricks like jumping and spinning on cue. However, many wild dolphins do the same thing. Marine scientists don't know why wild dolphins leap. Could it be that it is easier to move through air than water, and they are conserving energy? Maybe dolphins are trying to attract others in their pod. Most people would like to think they are just having fun!

Wild dolphins are playful marine mammals.

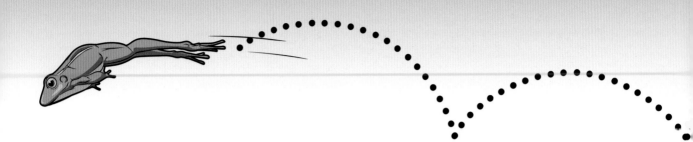

Leaping, bounding, hopping, jumping. Any way you say it; it's all about locomotion. Next time you come across a leaping animal, see if you can figure out why they move the way they do!

Glossary

aquatic (uh-KWAT-ik): having to do with water

breaching (BREECH-ing): rising and breaking the surface of water

carnivores (KAR-nuh-vorz): animals that eat other animals

habitat (HAB-uh-tat): the place where animals live

infertile (in-FER-tuhl): unable to grow plants

plankton (PLANGK-tuhn): tiny animals and plants that float in the ocean

predators (PRED-uh-turz): animals that hunt other animals for food

prey (PRAY): animals hunted by other animals for food

species (SPEE-sees): one certain kind of animal

swarm (SWORM): to move in large numbers

tendons (TEN-duhnz): strong bands of tissue that join muscle to bone

Index

Further Reading

Bonnett, John. *Big Cats*. Wildlife Education, 2003.

Ganeri, Anita. *Frogs and Tadpoles*. Smart apple Media, 2007.

Rebus, Anna. *Kangaroos.* Weigl Publishers, 2006.

Walker, Sally M. *Dolphins*. Lerner Publishing, 2007.

Websites

http://kids.nationalgeographic.com/

http://kidsgowild.com

http://www.naturesongs.com

About the Authors

David and Patricia Armentrout specialize in nonfiction children's books. They enjoy exploring different topics and have written about many subjects, including sports, animals, history, and people. David and Patricia love to spend their free time outdoors with their two boys and dog Max.